SPORTS INJURIES:
HOW TO PREVENT, DIAGNOSE, & TREAT

LACROSSE

Sports Injuries:
How to Prevent, Diagnose, & Treat

- Baseball
- Basketball
- Cheerleading
- Equestrian
- Extreme Sports
- Field
- Field Hockey
- Football
- Gymnastics
- Hockey
- Ice Skating
- Lacrosse
- Soccer
- Track
- Volleyball
- Weight Training
- Wrestling

**SPORTS INJURIES:
HOW TO PREVENT, DIAGNOSE, & TREAT**

LACROSSE

LISA McCOY

MASON CREST PUBLISHERS
www.masoncrest.com

Mason Crest Publishers Inc.
370 Reed Road
Broomall, PA 19008
(866) MCP-BOOK (toll free)
www.masoncrest.com

First printing

1 2 3 4 5 6 7 8 9 10

Library of Congress Cataloging-in-Publication Data on file
at the Library of Congress

ISBN 1-59084-636-2

Series ISBN 1-59084-625-7

Editorial and design by
Amber Books Ltd.
Bradley's Close
74–77 White Lion Street
London N1 9PF
www.amberbooks.co.uk

Project Editor: Michael Spilling
Design: Graham Curd
Picture Research: Natasha Jones

Printed and bound in the Hashemite Kingdom of Jordan

PICTURE CREDITS
Corbis: 6, 8, 10, 12, 15, 17, 18, 21, 23, 25, 26, 28, 36, 41, 43, 44, 46, 48, 50, 54, 56, 57, 58, 59; **Topham Picturepoint**: 38.

FRONT COVER: All Corbis.

ILLUSTRATIONS: Courtesy of Amber Books except:
Bright Star Publishing plc: 49, 53;
Tony Randell: 31, 33, 42.

CONTENTS

Foreword

Sports Injuries: How to Prevent, Diagnose, and Treat is a seventeen-volume series written for young people who are interested in learning about various sports and how to participate in them safely. Each volume examines the history of the sport and the rules of play; it also acts as a guide for prevention and treatment of injuries, and includes instruction on stretching, warming up, and strength training, all of which can help players avoid the most common musculoskeletal injuries. *Sports Injuries* offers ways for readers to improve their performance and gain more enjoyment from playing sports, and young athletes will find these volumes informative and helpful in their pursuit of excellence.

Sports medicine professionals assigned to a sport that they are not familiar with can also benefit from this series. For example, a football athletic trainer may need to provide medical care for a local gymnastics meet. Although the emergency medical principles and action plan would remain the same, the athletic trainer could provide better care for the gymnasts after reading a simple overview of the principles of gymnastics in *Sports Injuries*.

Although these books offer an overview, they are not intended to be comprehensive in the recognition and management of sports injuries. The text helps the reader appreciate and gain awareness of the common injuries possible during participation in sports. Reference material and directed readings are provided for those who want to delve further into the subject.

Written in a direct and easily accessible style, *Sports Injuries* is an enjoyable series that will help young people learn about sports and sports medicine.

Susan Saliba, Ph.D., National Athletic Trainers' Association Education Council

Professional lacrosse is a fast-growing sport in America: U.S. Lacrosse now boasts over 120,000 members.

History

Known as "the fastest sport on two feet" and popular across the world, lacrosse is also one of the oldest games known to man. Native American tribes in what is now the northeastern United States and southeastern Canada were playing the game long before French and English settlers arrived.

The Algonquins are known to have been the first tribe to play lacrosse. However, scholars are not certain which Native American tribe should be credited with actually inventing the game, and the Hurons and Iroquois may also have been involved in its birth.

The name "lacrosse" comes from the French for "cross" (la crosse), and indeed the stick used for the game is properly known as the "crosse." This derives from the fact that the sticks used by the Native Americans to play the game reminded the settlers of the **crosier** carried by French bishops. The name was coined in 1636 by a Jesuit missionary, Jean de Brebeuf, as he watched the Huron Indians play the game in an area near present-day Thunder Bay, Ontario, in Canada.

For today's version of the sport, which looks like a cross between hockey and rugby, teams have ten players each. When the Native Americans played it, however, teams could consist of hundreds of players; even teams of 1,000 or more were not unknown. Today, lacrosse is a formal game with specific rules, a designated playing field, specialized equipment, and so on. Again, this was not

Robert Wandas, of Rivider, N.Y., captain of the University of Pennsylvania Lacrosse team, poses with a lacrosse stick and protective gloves before a match in 1933.

the case with the Native Americans. Games could, and often did, range all over the countryside, with poles, rocks, or trees serving as goals—whatever was handy. Furthermore, games could last as long as two or three consecutive days, starting at dawn and ending at dusk.

Intertribal games of lacrosse, known as "baggataways," served a dual purpose. Not only were they a form of recreation, but they were also a means by which Native American warriors were trained. The long, tough, grueling conditions under which the games were played helped warriors develop strength, **stamina**,

Lacrosse was invented by the Native Americans and was seen as a valuable training tool for warriors.

and endurance. In fact, the Cherokees called lacrosse "the little brother of war" because of its military training value.

The first reported game between white French settlers and Native Americans took place in 1790. While no records of the game exist, one has to wonder if the settlers suffered a crushing defeat at the hands of experienced native players, for it was at least a hundred years before the next official game between settlers and Native Americans was recorded.

SETTLERS TAKE UP THE GAME

The game was officially "adopted" by the white settlers in 1834, when a group of Montreal businessmen made arrangements for the Caughnawaga Indians to play in Montreal. From there, the popularity of the game spread, and, in 1851, a group of white players finally succeeded in beating a team of Native Americans.

Montreal has the distinction of being the birthplace of modern lacrosse. The Montreal Lacrosse Club was formed in 1856, and immediate improvements in game play and equipment were developed. In 1867, the first official written rules were developed by Dr. W. George Beers, a dentist from Montreal, who founded the Canadian National Lacrosse Association. Beers' rules included a limit on the number of players allowed per team and the laying down of specific dimensions for the field of play. Also in that year, lacrosse was declared the official sport of the Dominion of Canada.

With its popularity established in Canada, lacrosse began to be played across the world. In 1867, a Native American team toured England, Ireland, France, and Scotland, and, in 1868, the English Lacrosse Association was formed. In the United States, a group of Native Americans demonstrated the game at the Saratoga Springs fairgrounds in New York in 1867, which led to the formation of the first official lacrosse club in that country: the Mohawk Club of Troy. In 1874, lacrosse was introduced in Australia, and, by 1878, it was being played in New Zealand. Intercollegiate lacrosse began in New York City at New York University. During the spring of 1881, Princeton and Columbia Universities also formed lacrosse teams. Harvard, Yale, and Johns Hopkins Universities soon followed. In 1882, Philips Andover Academy in Massachusetts, Philips Exeter Academy in New Hampshire, and the Lawrenceville School in New Jersey introduced the first high school lacrosse teams in the United States.

Since then, lacrosse has continued to grow and become more refined as a sport. In the United States alone, lacrosse is played at more than 500 colleges and universities, as well as at more than 1,400 high schools. Little-league lacrosse teams and women's lacrosse teams have emerged, and more than 100 colleges and universities, along with 150 high schools, currently sponsor programs.

Lacrosse was an official sport in the Olympic games in 1904 and 1908, with

Helmet with face guard, chest pads, and padded gloves are important protective gear, as demonstrated by this British schoolgirl player from 1938.

JIM BROWN—FOOTBALL AND LACROSSE PLAYER

Best known for his achievements as an athlete with the Cleveland Browns football team, Jim Brown was also an All-American lacrosse player. Of the game, Brown has been quoted as saying that on game day, football was his favorite sport, but, overall, he liked lacrosse better because it was more fun.

Canada taking home the gold medal both times. However, it was then dropped as an official sport. It was reinstated as a demonstration sport in 1928, 1932, and 1948, and another exhibition tournament was held at the Olympics in Los Angeles in 1980. As more and more countries worldwide take up this exciting, adrenaline-charged sport, it is hoped that lacrosse will once again be accepted as an official sport of the Olympics.

THE RULES OF THE GAME

What follows is no more than an outline of the rules of lacrosse. For more details, see www.laxrules.com.

The team

Each team has ten players: a goalkeeper, three defense, three midfielders, and three attack. Each team must keep at least four players, including the goalie, in its defensive half of the field and three in its offensive half. The midfielders may roam the entire field. Note that there are no boundaries to the field, but play stops if the ball enters an area that is unplayable or not clearly visible to the official.

Play

Play begins with a face-off: the ball is placed between the sticks of two players at the center of the field. At the whistle, each player tries to take possession, and, until one player has gained possession, only those players in the wing areas may move. Players pass and catch the ball, and may run with it in the stick. The only player whose hands may touch the ball is the goalkeeper.

The ball

A player may gain possession of the ball by dislodging it from an opponent's stick using a stick **check**, which includes the controlled poking and slapping of both the stick and the gloved hands of the player in possession of the ball.

When the ball is grounded, covering it with the back of a stick's net and preventing play by another player is prohibited.

Checking

Body checking is permitted if the opponent has the ball. However, all contact must occur from the front or side, and be above the waist and below the shoulders. Checking is prohibited when it is directed toward the face; is too close to the head or face; is uncontrolled; or involves holding down the other's stick.

An opponent's stick may also be checked if it is within 5 yards (4.5 m) of a loose ball or ball in the air.

The stick

Before the game begins, the officials check every stick for legality. The most common illegality in a stick is that its pocket is too deep. The strings at the bottom of the stick's head can be pulled to tighten the pocket.

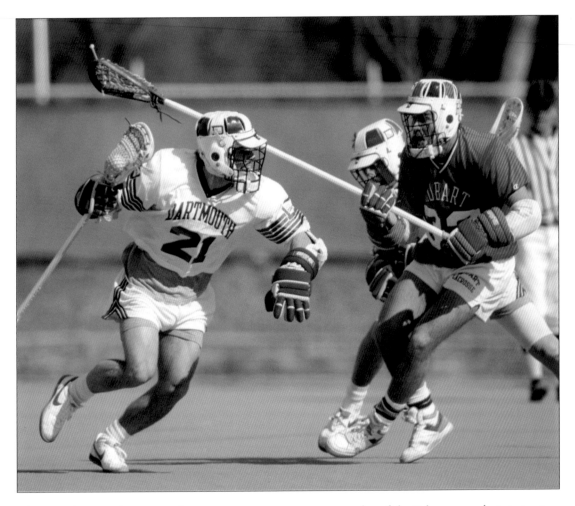

A lacrosse player on the Dartmouth team tries to maneuver past a member of the Hobart team who is trying to block him.

THE LEGEND OF LACROSSE

According to a Cherokee myth, the animals once challenged the birds to a game of ball. The animals took positions on the ground, while the birds took positions in the trees to await the throwing upward of the ball.

As the birds watched the game, two small creatures climbed up the tree where the leader of the birds was waiting, and asked if they could join the game. Taking

LEGENDARY LACROSSE PLAYERS

On October 1, 2000, four Onondaga Nation residents were accepted posthumously into the U.S. Lacrosse Hall of Fame. Known as "The Fabulous Four," Oren Lyons, Lyle Pierce, Stanley Pierce, and Irving Powless supported the game of lacrosse and kept its traditions alive among their people. Of particular interest is the fact that they played against Johns Hopkins University in the tryouts for the Olympic Games in 1932.

one look at these tiny creatures, the leader of the birds saw that they were four-footed and asked why they did not go to the animals' side, where they belonged. The creatures replied that they had already done so, but had been laughed at and sent away because they were so small.

The leader of the birds felt sorry for the tiny creatures and wanted to let them play, but there was one problem: how could they join the birds' team when they had no wings? After discussing it, the birds decided to try to make wings for them. The leather head of a drum was cut up and used to make wings. These were attached to the legs of one of the creatures, and so the first bat was created.

The ball was tossed up, and the bat was told to catch it. His swiftness in dodging and circling about, keeping the ball constantly in motion and never letting it fall to the ground, soon convinced the birds that they had indeed made a wise decision.

They then turned their attention to the other little creature, but realized that all the leather had been used up in making wings for the bat. The birds decided that wings might be made by stretching out the creature's skin. Two large birds seized him on each side with their strong bills and tugged and pulled at his fur until the skin between his front feet and his hind feet was stretched, and so the first flying squirrel was created. The leader of the birds threw the ball into the air, and the flying squirrel gracefully sprang off the limb to catch the ball in his teeth, and then sailed through the air to another tree a hundred feet away.

These two tiny creatures were so successful in dodging and flying, and keeping the ball out of the hands of even the fastest animals, that they scored many goals for the birds, ultimately winning the game for them. After that, in honor of their invaluable help during the game, Cherokee players tied a small piece of the bat's wing to their lacrosse sticks for luck.

Cherokee lacrosse players tied small pieces of bat's wing to their lacrosse sticks for luck in honor of the legend describing the origins of the game.

Mental Preparation

Everyone understands the importance of being physically prepared to play a sport. However, just as important is mental preparation, which can often make the difference between a good lacrosse player and a great one.

VISUALIZATION

Visualization is a form of mental preparation familiar to people in all walks of life: athletes, actors, musicians, writers, businesspeople, and everyone in between. Although a well-used tool today, visualization was not always known to people in the Western world. For a long time, Western philosophy assumed that the mind and the body were two separate, distinct entities. This was in direct opposition to Eastern philosophies, which have maintained for centuries that there is a deep, profound connection between the body and the mind. What you think or how you feel has a direct correlation to your body. Likewise, how your body feels, or the messages it sends to your brain, affects your mental state. Take advantage of the link between your mind and the body when you are mentally preparing yourself for anything in life, whether it be a big lacrosse game or a big test.

Visualization might sound hard, but it is easy to do. To visualize, picture yourself performing an activity correctly, without injury or mistake. For example, if you are concerned about an upcoming lacrosse game in which you will be goalkeeper, you should close your eyes and picture yourself blocking shot after

One player challenges another in a fast-paced, competitive game at the University of Maryland. The player in red is wearing a mouth guard to protect her teeth.

shot. Then, when it comes to the actual game, the fact that you have rehearsed your athletic performance in your mind's eye lets you have the confidence you need to give it your all.

ATTITUDE

Attitude—the mindset with which you approach something—can often make the difference in your game play. As much as possible, you should try to maintain a positive attitude. Granted, there will be times during a rough practice or a losing game when it will be hard to maintain a positive attitude, but, if you can manage it, a positive attitude or mindset can help you keep things in perspective.

Attitude also has a lot to do with the focus and level of concentration that you bring to a game. Visualization can help in this area too. By visualizing what it is you want to achieve as a lacrosse player, your concentration and the determination to make your visions a reality can lead to an improved attitude. Sometimes, too, pep talks by coaches, inspirational sayings, or stories shared by other players can help you to keep a positive attitude. It is important to stay focused: your teammates will be counting on you to give the game your full attention.

You should also bring an attitude of fun to any game or practice. Above all, sporting events are designed to be fun for the players and the spectators alike. Yes, you should take every game seriously, but it is important to keep in mind that winning or losing is less important than having fun and practicing good sportsmanship.

DRILLS

Drills are a series of exercises designed to build specific skills. In lacrosse, different drills are designed to help players develop better ball handling, stick handling, and eye–hand coordination, which is a crucial skill to have in this sport.

Drills are a good way to foster teamwork and cooperation among players, as well as those all-important lacrosse skills that are central to the game.

There are also drills based on the individual positions. The following are examples of exercises for both offensive and defensive positions and are provided by the American Sport Education Program.

DRILLS FOR OFFENSE

- The first offensive drill builds the skill of cradling, which refers to the movement of the stick in a semicircular pattern, thereby creating a **centrifugal** force that keeps the ball in the pocket of the stick. The drill is popularly known as "Rock-a-Bye-Baby."

Sit on the ground cross-legged and hold the stick with the top hand just below the pocket and the other hand halfway down the shaft of the stick. Extend the stick at an angle of about 45° away from the body. Rock the ball from side to side, like you are rocking a baby, moving not more than 12 inches (30 cm) in total—in other words, about 6 inches (15 cm) to each side. As you gain strength and confidence, try moving faster or holding the stick more vertically. You can also try holding the stick just on one side of the body and rocking back and forth.

- The next drill develops your skills in passing, and you will need a partner. Begin by standing about 30 feet (9 m) apart from one another. Pass the ball back and forth, concentrating on maintaining the proper form when catching and throwing.

  As a variation, you can practice catching with your nondominant hand: for example, if you are right-handed, try throwing and catching with your left hand. Or, you can throw with your right hand and catch with your left.

- The third drill works on your skills in dodging—the sudden change in movement of the stick and ball in an effort to keep it away from an opponent. There are three basic dodges in lacrosse: the face dodge, the roll dodge, and the bull dodge. The face dodge is used when you are being rushed at head-on by another player; the roll dodge is used when another player is trying to swing at or check your stick; the bull dodge is used when another player is standing still.

  For this drill, you need 4–6 lacrosse players. Everyone should stand in a line, with one person standing about 15 feet (4.5 m) from the line of other players. This person is the only one with the ball. To start, the person in front calls out the type of dodge he intends to execute, then runs down the line of players, weaving in and out while performing dodges until the end of the line is reached. At this point, the ball is given to the player at the end of the line, who moves in front of the row, calls out the intended dodge, and moves through the line. This pattern is continued until everyone has had a turn.

- This last offensive drill develops scooping, which is exactly what it sounds like: scooping up the loose ball and returning it to play on the field.

  For this drill, you will need another player. Stand facing each other, about 30 feet (9 m) apart. Start with the ball at your feet. Scoop it up, then pass it to your partner. Concentrate on maintaining the proper form for both

Teamwork and communication among lacrosse players are important skills to develop at the same time as you are working on your lacrosse-playing technique.

scooping and catching. After catching the ball, your partner should run a few steps and then pass the ball back to you. Take turns starting with the ball at each other's feet. For a variation, try scooping with your nondominant hand or alternate between your dominant and nondominant hands.

DRILLS FOR DEFENSE

• The first defensive drill works on the skill of body checking. This is when you, as a defender, move in the same direction as the person who is carrying the ball, with your body positioned in such a way that it blocks the player from moving in the direction she wants to go.

In this drill, you will need a partner and a space about 30 feet (9 m) wide and 60 feet (18 m) long. One person should have the ball. Starting at the beginning of the 60-foot mark, the person with the ball should run the length of this area. The partner, who is acting as the defender, should follow, running alongside and concentrating on maintaining proper body position and footwork at the same time. The defender should try to remain on only one side of the ball carrier the whole time. Take turns being the ball carrier and the defender.

• Footwork is an important skill in lacrosse, especially in defense. You will need coordination as you run around the field, passing and catching the ball, but you will also have to focus on dodging and checking other players. The following drill is aimed at building your fundamental footwork skills.

Place your lacrosse stick on the ground, horizontally in front of you. Step over the stick with one foot, then the next. Then, step backward with the second foot, and follow with the first. The movement should feel like you are running in place over your stick. Concentrate on keeping your knees high.

One of the key aspects of being a good lacrosse player is being able to remain completely focused on the game no matter what takes place. Here a goalie defends his goal in a game at College Park, Maryland.

After a few minutes of this, with the stick still horizontal in front of you, squat down slightly and slide to the side of the stick. Step forward so you are in front of it, then slide to the other side of the stick and step back behind it. Essentially, you are performing a sliding motion around your stick. Perform this movement for a few minutes.

Then, with the stick vertical in front of you, jump over it with both feet, and then jump back to the other side. Keep jumping back and forth over the stick for a few minutes, making sure that your knees are lifted high in the air when you jump.

Finally, take several lacrosse sticks, cones, tires, or whatever you can find that is handy, and place the objects in two lines, about 1 ft. (30 cm.) apart. Step forward between the objects with your knees as high as possible. This drill should feel and look a lot like the drill you see football players performing when they run along a row of tires, placing each foot in the middle of the tire.

- The next drill works on stick checking, the repeated tapping motion a defender uses to dislodge the ball from an opponent's stick. This drill, known as "Woody Woodpecker," helps teach the motion and control necessary for stick checking.

While winning is certainly a wonderful feeling, it is important to treat all players with respect and to concentrate on having fun. After all, it's just a game.

ADVICE FROM PLAYERS

- **Concentrate on having fun and on the game, no matter what.**
- **Approach the game as a goalie would: one shot at a time.**
- **Pay attention to the ball and talk to your teammates.**
- **Play the ball no matter who has it or where it is.**
- **Respect your opponents. Be polite and practice good etiquette at all times.**
- **Treat everyone—coaches, officials, other players—with respect.**

Source: www.LaxTips.com

You will need a partner for this exercise. One person should hold his stick horizontal to the ground, anywhere from hip to shoulder level, and the other person should hit the "opponent's" stick with his stick, using firm and rapid tapping motions, just like a woodpecker tapping on a tree. Try this in different positions, such as behind, forward, and to each side. When done, switch roles and repeat.

- The final defensive drill is a blocking drill known as "Monkey in the Middle." You will need two other people to carry out this drill. Two people should stand facing each other about 30 feet (9 m) apart. As the first person throws the ball to the second person, the person in the middle (the "monkey") should attempt to block the pass. If the monkey is successful in this attempt, the monkey takes possession. If unsuccessful, the monkey must quickly run around the first person and then head for the second person, trying to block the shot again. Basically, it's just like a game of keep-away. Be sure to take turns alternating who is the monkey.

Warm-Up Exercises

Before playing "the fastest sport on two feet," it is extremely important that you take the time to properly stretch and warm up your muscles. Lacrosse is a tough, intensive sport, with lots of running, throwing, and jostling. If you do not take the time to warm up, you may seriously injure yourself.

According to lacrosse coach Bob Scott, a typical college game will involve a high number of plays, with the two teams taking seventy-five to eighty-five shots at the goal between them, and scoring about fifteen to twenty-five goals. Such an extremely fast game needs quick reflexes, as well as quick wits, so take the time to warm up, even when it seems like a hassle.

The following sections will provide a sample of warm-up exercises from head to toe, along with a few exercises which are specific to the sport of lacrosse. Your lacrosse coach will also probably have some good ideas for stretches and warm-up exercises. When you are performing stretches, it is important to keep a few things in mind:

- Each stretch should be held for a minimum of ten seconds. You can increase your flexibility by holding the stretches for longer periods of time—say, twenty to thirty seconds.
- Do not bounce or jerk your muscles when you are stretching. This can lead to tearing or spraining of the muscles.

Lacrosse is such a fast-paced sport that players should always take the time to ensure that their muscles are properly warmed up in order to avoid injury.

- Do not rush through your stretches. This does your body no good and can lead to injury. Always take the time to warm up properly.
- Listen to your body and respect your limits. A small amount of discomfort is expected when stretching. If something causes you excessive pain, stop immediately. Do not compare your stretching ability to anyone else's. Everyone has their own particular abilities and limits.
- Lacrosse is an intensive sport with a lot of running, so it is a good idea to begin and end each warm-up session with five to ten minutes of light jogging. This gives your muscles the opportunity they need to warm up or cool down.

Neck

1. This exercise is designed to stretch the neck muscles from side to side. Stand with your legs shoulder-width apart. Tuck your chin into your chest and hold for ten to twenty seconds.

Tilt your right ear toward your right shoulder, and hold for ten to twenty seconds. Return to center. Tilt the left ear toward the left shoulder, and again hold for ten to twenty seconds.

Repeat three times on each side.

2. This exercise stretches the neck muscles by rotating them gently. First, stand with your feet shoulder-width apart. Slowly rotate your head to the right, and look over your right shoulder until you feel a gentle stretch. Hold for ten to twenty seconds.

Now bring the head to face forward again, then rotate the neck to the left, looking over the left shoulder until you feel a gentle stretch. Again hold for ten to twenty seconds.

Shoulders and arms

Lacrosse is a sport in which a lot of throwing and catching take place, so it is important that you take the time to thoroughly stretch your arms and shoulders:

1. Stand with your feet shoulder-width apart. Raise both arms above your head and bend the left elbow, then grasp it with the right hand. Pull your left upper arm gently toward the middle of your body. You should feel this stretch in your triceps muscle. Hold for ten to twenty seconds.

Raise your arms above your head again, then bend the right elbow and grasp it with your left hand. Pull your right upper arm gently toward the middle of your body until you feel a gentle stretch in your triceps. Hold for ten to twenty seconds.

2. Stand with your feet shoulder-width apart. Clasp your hands behind your back, with your elbows fully extended. Lift your arms slightly and bend over at the waist, then lift your arms up even farther, if you are able to do so, and hold this stretch for ten to twenty seconds.

Repeat four more times.

To stretch your shoulder and chest muscles, stand with your feet shoulder-width apart. Clasp your hands behind your back with your elbows fully extended. Then raise your arms as high as you can until you feel a gentle stretch. Hold for ten to twenty seconds.

Legs and ankles

In lacrosse, sprained ankles, groin pulls, and **hamstring** and **quadriceps** strains are common injuries. To prevent these injuries, try the following exercises.

1. This exercise works on your hamstrings. Sit on the floor with your legs stretched straight out in front of you. Your feet should be about hip-width apart. Keep your legs as straight as possible, then reach forward and grab hold of either your ankles or toes, depending on your level of flexibility. Hold for ten to twenty seconds. You should feel this stretch in the backs of the knees and your lower back. Try it with your toes pointing straight up and with your toes pointing forward.

2. For another seated hamstring stretch, sit with your legs spread wide apart. Lean over your left leg, and grab hold of the toes of your left foot or ankle. Point your toes forward and hold for ten to twenty seconds, then point your toes up and hold for another ten to twenty seconds. Sit up. Turn so that you are facing the center, and then lean over your right leg, grabbing hold of the toes of your right foot or ankle. Point your toes forward and hold for ten to twenty seconds, then point your toes up and hold for ten to twenty seconds.

3. This will stretch your quadriceps. Stand with your feet shoulder-width apart. Grab hold of your right ankle, and pull it behind you toward your buttocks, bending the knee. You may need to hold onto a chair or a wall for balance. Hold this stretch for ten to twenty seconds. Repeat with the left leg.

4. Known as the butterfly stretch, this works the groin muscles. Sit on the floor with your knees bent and the soles of your feet pressed together. Hold your feet with your

A calf stretch is essential preparation for any lacrosse game or training session.

hands, then rest your elbows on your lower legs. Lean forward and try to touch your forehead to the floor while you press down on your legs. Hold for ten to twenty seconds.

5. To stretch your calves, stand facing a wall, and place your hands at about shoulder height. Place one foot in front of the other, keeping the heel of your back foot firmly on the floor. Place your weight on your forward, bent leg, and then lean forward, as if you are trying to push against the wall. Hold for ten to twenty seconds.

Repeat for the other leg.

6. For the second calf stretch, you need a flight of stairs or a sturdy box. First, line up your heels with the edge of the step. Then move your feet back so that the balls of your feet are on the edge of the step and the rest of your feet are hanging off the edge. (You may need to lean against something or hold on to a railing for balance.) Slowly dip your heels down, then come back up. Repeat ten times.

7. This stretch works your ankles. Stand with your legs shoulder-width apart. Point your right toe so that it is touching the ground, and roll your ankle in a clockwise direction three times. Then roll the ankle counterclockwise three times.

Repeat for the left foot.

SPECIAL EXERCISES FOR LACROSSE PLAYERS

According to Kurtis Shultz, who currently works as a trainer with Team Toyota, the Baltimore Thunder, and the Loyola men's and women's lacrosse teams, there are some basic exercises that can be of tremendous benefit to lacrosse players. For the different positions on the teams, Shultz recommends specific exercises, and advises that they be performed regularly.

Defenders will be pushing attackers off their body, so they need strong triceps and strong pectoral, or chest, muscles. Attackers will be using pushing motions when facing off and also to secure elbow room and move around in a crush. Shultz recommends the inclined-press exercise to develop strong triceps and chest muscles:

1. To perform an inclined press, lie on a weight bench that is at an angle; your shoulders should be higher than your buttocks. The weight bar should be supported on rests at a level with your chest. Grasp the weight bar with both hands and lift the weight over your forehead and then back to your chest. Repeat ten to fifteen times.

It is a good idea to have a **spotter** standing over you while you lift the weight, to make sure that you

Crunches will help strengthen your abdominal muscles. For a more extreme crunch exercise, bring both knees up together, at the same time raising your head to meet them. Hold the position for six to ten seconds, then relax.

do not accidentally drop it on yourself or so that the weight can be lifted off you if you are too tired to continue.

For all players, says Shultz, a strong midsection and strong abdominals are essential. To Shultz, crunches are the key to abdominal development, especially oblique crunches:

2. To perform an oblique crunch, lie on your back with your knees bent and feet on the floor, and with your hands behind your head. Next twist your legs to the right and lower your knees to the floor. With your lower body in this position, raise your upper body so that your shoulders come off the floor. Repeat ten to twenty times. Then, twist your legs to the left and lower your knees to the floor. Repeat the crunching movement on the right side of the body ten to twenty times.

Shultz also stresses the importance of shoulder exercises. Not only are strong shoulders essential for skilled stick work, but shooting, checking, facing off, and other movements in lacrosse are motions that need the benefit of strong shoulders as well. Furthermore, strong shoulder muscles can help to prevent injuries to the **rotator cuff**.

3. A great exercise for developing shoulders is the military press. Hold a set of dumbbells weighing 5–10 pounds (2–4.5 kg) at shoulder height, with your palms facing forward. Raise the dumbbells above your head, twisting your hand at the same time, so that, at the end of the movement, your palms are facing each other over the top of your head. Then lower the weights back to shoulder level, twisting again so that the palms are facing forward. Perform this action ten to fifteen times.

WATER, WATER, WATER

When you are playing a sport, you sweat, thereby losing water. As a result, your body becomes dehydrated. Dehydration can seriously affect your athletic performance: you may tire faster and have less stamina, and your muscles may even feel weak. Drink plenty of water during breaks between warm-ups and games, to make sure that your body stays properly hydrated.

Of course, drinking plenty of water is even more important when you are playing in hot or humid weather. During warm weather, cool water

is a better choice for you than freezing cold or warm water. Drinking very cold water may cause your muscles to cramp because of the sudden effort that your already tired muscles will have to make to warm up the water. As for warm fluids, these are absorbed less quickly than cool water, and cool water is itself more likely to help cool off your overheated body.

Remember to drink plenty of water, both during practices and games themselves, to keep your body well-hydrated.

The last exercise Shultz recommends is wrist-strengthening exercise, to benefit stick work. A great strengthening exercise is the wrist curl:

4. Sit in a chair with your knees bent. Hold a dumbbell weighing 1–3 pounds (0.5–1.5 kg) in one hand, palm facing down, and with your forearm on your thigh. Slowly bend your wrist upward as far as possible. Hold for ten to twenty seconds, then lower the wrist slowly, keeping your forearm on your thigh. Repeat ten times. Then repeat for the other hand.

Next, hold the dumbbell with your palm facing down and your forearm on your thigh. Slowly bend the wrist as far as possible and hold for ten to twenty seconds, and then lower slowly. Repeat ten times. Then repeat for the other hand.

Lacrosse players should strengthen their wrists and forearms by performing special lifts with light dumb bells. You can perform these lifts by resting your arms on either your knees or a bench.

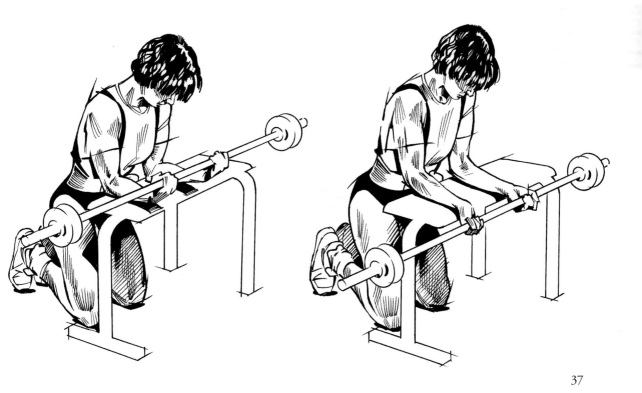

Equipment

At its most basic, lacrosse is a game that requires only two pieces of equipment: a ball and a stick. However, for safety and protection, there are several other pieces of equipment that must be considered.

Men's lacrosse is traditionally a rough game, and helmets are required for all players. In women's lacrosse, however, only the goalie must wear a helmet. In the light of recent studies, it seems apparent that this ruling needs to be reexamined.

According to an article published by the Center for Neuro Skills (C.N.S.), "high rates of head and face injuries among women and the increasing numbers of children learning to play lacrosse … is prompting another look at how much protective gear they need." A second study, conducted by the University of Virginia, discovered that "injuries to the head and face were significantly more prevalent among females (30.1 percent of all injuries) than among males (18 percent of all injuries), and often resulted from contact with the ball." Furthermore, "children ages four to eleven years old experienced the highest percent of injuries to the head and face of all lacrosse players."

Clearly, lacrosse is a game in which safety must be considered a priority.

THE STICK

While there are guidelines and rules with regards to players' sticks, there is a lot of leeway here. The "right" lacrosse stick is, ultimately, the one that is best for your

A lacrosse player wears goggles to protect her eyes in a women's lacrosse game in Syracuse, New York.

SAFETY EQUIPMENT

For men, the following safety equipment is recommended:

- helmet with attached mouth guard;
- rib pads, shoulder pads, and elbow pads;
- padded gloves;
- protective cup/jock strap;
- shoes with cleats.

For women, the only recommended equipment is:

- mouth guard;
- padded gloves;
- shoes with cleats.

Female goalkeepers should also wear the following additional pieces of safety equipment:

- helmet with attached face guard, throat protector, and mouth guard;
- chest protector;
- arm pads and leg pads.

age, sex, position, and ability. For men, lacrosse sticks usually have an aluminum handle with either a traditional or a mesh pocket: a traditional pocket is made of nylon and leather; a mesh pocket consists of woven nylon webbing. The depth of the pocket can vary, and the typical length of a men's lacrosse stick is 30–60 inches

The goalie pictured to the right is wearing the standard safety items required by lacrosse regulations: helmet with face guard; arm, shoulder, and chest pads, and padded gloves.

A typical lacrosse stick includes various essential features:

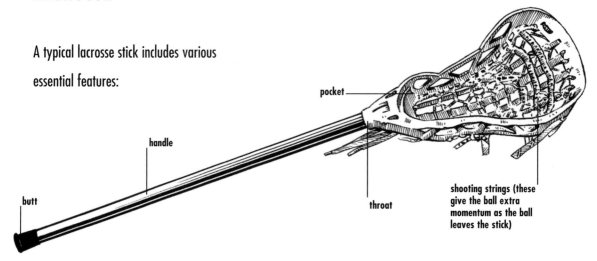

pocket

handle

butt

throat

shooting strings (these give the ball extra momentum as the ball leaves the stick)

(76–152 cm), depending on the position played and personal preference. For women, lacrosse sticks have either a wood or aluminum handle and a traditional pocket, which is shallower than the pocket used by men. The pocket of a women's lacrosse stick must have four or five leather thongs and no more than two shooting strings. The typical length of the stick is 36–44 inches (91–111 cm).

THE HELMET

Lacrosse, in general, is an intense sport in which players are constantly checking each other and running the risk of injury from other player's sticks. It only makes good sense to wear a helmet. Ideally, the lacrosse helmet should provide full protection to the face and the neck. Furthermore, lacrosse face guards must meet certain standards. For example, the wire mesh of the guard must protect the face, but not be too close to the face. This is so that the guard does not smash into the face in the case of a full-face collision. In addition, the chin strap must be padded to protect the face in case of a collision with another player.

Mouth guards are often attached to the helmet directly, but can be sold as a separate item. Mouth guards serve to protect the teeth and cushion blows to the

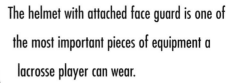

The helmet with attached face guard is one of the most important pieces of equipment a lacrosse player can wear.

head, thereby protecting against **concussion**. Mouth guards come preformed and eventually mold to the mouth with use.

SHOES

Lacrosse shoes are much the same for women and men. They are similar to a football or soccer shoe, in that they have **cleats**. These cleats enable players to get better traction on the field, but they can also lead to injury if a player is not careful. Long cleats provide better grip, but can lead to knee injuries: if the foot becomes firmly fixed in the playing surface, a twisting motion or impact from another player may force the knee joint beyond its normal range of motion.

Common Injuries and Treatment

Lacrosse is a contact sport, and the potential for injury is similar to sports such as hockey or rugby. A proper warm-up helps prevent injury, but injuries can and do happen, commonly to the hands and wrists, shoulders, thighs, and knees.

HAND AND WRIST INJURIES

Injuries to the hand and wrist suffered by lacrosse players include **fractures**, **dislocations**, and sprains. These can occur as a result of a player falling to the ground, getting hit on the hand by another player's stick, or colliding with another player.

There are several different types of fractures, categorized according to their makeup and severity. A doctor can tell you specifically what kind of a fracture you may have. Typically, a fracture is not something you can treat yourself. Until you can consult a physician, the usual treatment is to keep the injured area immobile and apply an ice pack for twenty to thirty minutes. According to Dr. Allan M. Levy, team physician for the New York Giants football team, "many finger fractures are not serious, especially those in the tip of the finger … Taping an injured finger to the healthy one next to it usually allows you to return to activity." However, Dr. Levy also notes that if the fracture occurs in the second or third finger bone, a **splint** may be required, in which case it can take four to six weeks for the fracture to heal completely.

Looking like a combination of field hockey and rugby, but with a style all its own, lacrosse is a sport in which the potential for injury can be high—even when you have warmed up properly.

A finger may be dislocated if it is struck with a great deal of force, either by a player or a player's equipment. Common symptoms can include pain, a loss of mobility in the finger, and a noticeable deformity in the joint. Do not try to force the joint back into place yourself—you can potentially cause more damage. Instead, Dr. Levy recommends that you tape the dislocated finger to the healthy one next to it and consider icing the area for periods of twenty to thirty minutes. Consult a physician to arrange for X-rays as soon as possible. These will determine the severity of the injury and establish whether there are fractures. Typically, you will have to wear a splint to immobilize the joint. Usually, recovery time is anywhere from six to twelve weeks.

A sprain occurs when **ligaments** are stretched or torn. Finger sprains can occur when a lacrosse player receives a blow to the end of a finger or if the finger joints are forced beyond their normal range of motion, which might happen if a player falls to the ground or bumps against another player with great force. Typical symptoms include pain, swelling, and loss of mobility. This is not something that you should treat by yourself. Keep the joint immobile by taping it to a healthy finger and apply ice for twenty-minute intervals until you can consult a physician. In most cases,

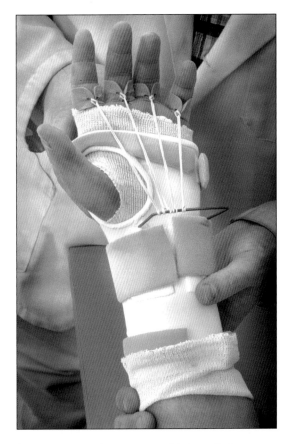

It is important to keep an injured joint or limb immobile so that the injury heals properly.

treatment may consist of keeping the finger in a splint for two weeks. After that, it will be taped to a healthy finger until the injury is completely healed and full mobility is restored.

Lacrosse is a sport in which players often have to perform quick "snap-and-twist" motions when they quickly catch the ball and throw it to another player. As a result, a common wrist injury that players can suffer is a strain brought about by simple overuse.

SHOULDERS

Shoulder injuries can be common in lacrosse players, primarily for two reasons. Shoulder injuries are often

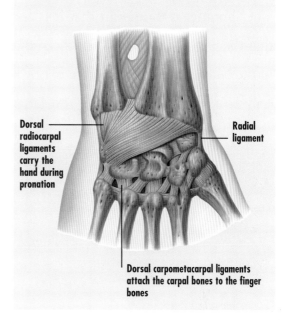

WRIST LIGAMENTS

By strengthening the muscles of the wrist, you can help prevent injuries such as wrist strains.

Dorsal radiocarpal ligaments carry the hand during pronation

Radial ligament

Dorsal carpometacarpal ligaments attach the carpal bones to the finger bones

overuse injuries and can occur as a result of the constant twisting and throwing motions that players engage in during the course of a game. Shoulder injuries are also common due to players being struck with a lacrosse stick or landing heavily on a shoulder as a player falls to the ground.

Common shoulder injuries often seen in lacrosse players include fractures, dislocations, sprains, and **contusions**. Fractures in the shoulder area almost always affect the collarbone, usually in the middle. A lacrosse player might suffer a fractured collarbone by receiving a direct hit to it, falling on it, or falling with outstretched arms. A fractured collarbone is a serious injury. If you suspect such an injury, keep the arm still: immobilize it in a sling, and wrap a bandage around the arm so that it is kept close to the body. Ice may be applied for twenty-minute intervals until a doctor can be seen. Typical recovery time is anywhere from six to twelve weeks.

Shoulder instability

The shoulder is unique in that it is a shallow ball-and-socket joint, which means that the joint is not very stable. According to Dr. Levy, the shoulder is the only joint in the body that is not held together by its ligaments. Rather, the few ligaments serve only to keep it from moving too far in any one direction. For that very reason,

The lacrosse player seen here on the right is wearing a knee brace to help support a knee that has been injured. The player on the left has suffered a nasty fall that could damage her knee or ankle.

shoulder dislocations are common among lacrosse players. The ball at the top of the upper arm bone comes out of the socket in the shoulder blade, and symptoms include an obvious deformity of the shoulder, extreme pain, muscle **spasms**, and loss of mobility. Again, you should not try to force the shoulder joint back in place or have anyone else try to do it for you. Instead, place your arm in a sling and ice the affected area for twenty-minute intervals, until you can consult a doctor.

These shoulder injuries are often caused by accidents, which, by definition, are difficult to prevent. The most important measure is to learn how to fall properly. Too often, when a person falls, the natural inclination is to hold out the arms in order to break the fall. This action, however, can lead to the very shoulder injuries just described. Instead, tuck in and roll with the fall rather than trying to break it. Your lacrosse coach or your doctor should be able to give you further instruction in this area. Shoulder pads are also a good way to lessen the impact of a fall or blow to the shoulder.

THIGHS

Common thigh injuries suffered by lacrosse players can include strains, bruises, and fractures. Particularly common are injuries to the hamstrings and quadriceps.

The hamstrings cause the knee to bend and the thigh to move backward relative to the body. Hamstrings play a vital role in walking, running, jumping, and controlling movement. A hamstring strain is one of the most common injuries and one of the most **debilitating** as this is such a large muscle group. Typical symptoms of a hamstring pull can include sharp pain and swelling, and, in the most severe tears, bruising due to internal bleeding within the muscle. You may also be unable to raise your leg straight off the ground more than a short distance without feeling pain. Typical treatment includes rest, ice, and compression: usually, resting for at

MINOR INJURIES

Cuts

- Grab the cleanest material you can find, such as a washcloth or a strip of gauze.
- Cover the cut with the cloth, and apply firm pressure to the wound. Maintain this pressure until the bleeding has stopped.
- Next, clean the wound gently with an antiseptic and spread a thin layer of antibiotic ointment over the wound.
- If you cannot control the bleeding within a few minutes, seek medical help.

Bruises

- Apply a cold compress or ice pack to the bruised area as soon as possible. Leave in place for fifteen minutes. Repeat several times a day to alleviate the pain and prevent swelling.

Sprains

- Immediately immerse the sprained area in ice water, or apply an ice pack for twenty minutes, to control the swelling. Repeat at twenty-minute intervals over a period of at least four hours until swelling has stopped.
- Elevate the sprained limb to at least waist level to help alleviate swelling.
- Once the swelling has stopped, soak the sprained area three times a day—first in warm water for twenty minutes, then in icy water for twenty minutes.

Source: Frandsen, Betty Rae, Kathryn J. Frandsen, and Kent P. Frandsen. Where's Mom Now That I Need Her? *Sandy, UT: Aspen West Publishing Company, 1983.*

least two or three days; icing the muscle for twenty minutes, three to four times a day; and wrapping the muscle in a **compression bandage**.

Symptoms of a quadriceps injury include a sudden, stabbing pain in the front of the thigh; tenderness or possible discoloration on the front of the thigh; and pain when trying to straighten the knee. Typical treatment includes resting the injury for several days, icing to reduce swelling, wearing a compression bandage, then a gentle stretching program to strengthen the muscles.

THE KNEE

The knee is a complex joint. It is an intricate network of muscle, tendons, ligaments, cartilage, and bone, which assists us in a variety of motions. Knee sprains are among the most common knee injuries seen in lacrosse players, and the recommended method of treatment is the familiar regimen of resting, icing, and compressing the knee.

The information in this chapter is not intended to replace the advice of your coach or physician. For further reading, however, you may wish to consult *The Sports Medicine Bible* or the website MedTerms.com, which features a medical dictionary.

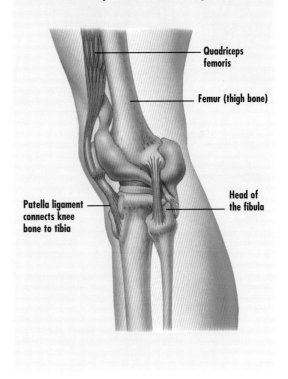

STRUCTURE OF THE KNEE

One of our body's more unique joints, the knee helps us to move in so many different ways.

Quadriceps femoris

Femur (thigh bone)

Head of the fibula

Patella ligament connects knee bone to tibia

Careers in Lacrosse

For a career in lacrosse, you can choose to play professionally or become a coach. This chapter will explore the ways in which these two career goals can be achieved, as well as provide a listing of some colleges and organizations that are known for their lacrosse programs or scholarships.

PROFESSIONAL LACROSSE PLAYER

There are several organizations and leagues for professional lacrosse teams, among them the Professional Lacrosse Players Association, the National Lacrosse League, and the Ontario Lacrosse Association. These are often separated into divisions according to the geographical location of each team. Although many professional sports leagues have existed for almost a century now, the sport of professional lacrosse is still in its infancy. According to Peter Schmitz, president of the Professional Lacrosse Players Association, things are changing, however, and he is confident that "this sport will become the next big sport in North America. It has all the ingredients that draw fan interest: games are high-scoring, physical, fast, action-packed, and skilled."

So how does one go about becoming a professional lacrosse player? The answer is, in much the same way that one becomes a professional hockey or baseball player. Unfortunately, at the time of this writing, there are no professional lacrosse teams for women. Hopefully, as lacrosse continues to gain popularity, this will soon change. For women interested in pursuing a career in lacrosse, coaching a high school or college women's team is an option.

College lacrosse is growing in popularity thanks to its fast action, high scoring potential, and excitement.

For many young men, the path to becoming a professional lacrosse player begins in high school or college. Obviously, having some talent is of great benefit to the budding professional, but hard work, determination, and regular practice can go a long way: an 'okay' player may become a good player, and a good player a great player. The key to becoming proficient is practice, practice, practice. Part of becoming a professional lacrosse player means finding a college that has a renowned or prestigious team. Many colleges offer lacrosse scholarships, and several, especially on the East Coast of the United States, have been known for decades for their outstanding collegiate lacrosse teams. Talk to your school's guidance counselor, visit the career center at your library, or talk to lacrosse coaches at the colleges you are

College lacrosse is growing fast in the United States. The United States defeated Canada, 18–15, for its sixth straight ILF World Championship on July 14, 2002, in Perth, Australia.

For many lacrosse players, their love of the game begins at an early age — perhaps ten or eleven — and can continue right through high school and college.

considering to find out about available scholarships. Schools offering scholarships include Johns Hopkins, Princeton, Rutgers, and the University of Maryland.

PROFESSIONAL LACROSSE COACH

As with many professional athletes, a career as a professional lacrosse player can be relatively short. The sport places an enormous toll on your body, and even those in the best of shape find that, sooner or later, their body has had enough. Or, a player might suffer an injury on the playing field that is so severe he is unable to continue playing professional lacrosse.

However, this does not mean that a career in lacrosse is over. Often, those who were lacrosse players in college, or even former professional lacrosse players, stay involved in the sport by becoming a coach. Furthermore, lacrosse coaches are needed for a wide range of ages, from middle school all the way up through college and into the pros.

If you decide that you want to be a lacrosse coach, consider taking courses in **anatomy**, **physiology**, and physical education, because lacrosse coaches sometimes have to quickly assess and treat injuries on the field. In addition, consider getting a teaching certificate with a concentration in physical education, since many lacrosse coaches in schools and universities are also teachers.

Johns Hopkins University (the players wearing white) and Syracuse University (the players wearing orange) are two schools with well-known lacrosse programs that offer scholarships to prospective students.

C.O.A.C.H.

The acronym C.O.A.C.H. sums up the qualities of an effective lacrosse coach:

Many lacrosse players go on to become lacrosse coaches.

C—COMPREHENSION: An effective lacrosse coach thoroughly understands the ins and outs of the game and clearly communicates skills, rules, and game tactics to the players.

O—OUTLOOK: An effective lacrosse coach has a clear set of coaching objectives and goals. The most common ones are to have fun, to help players develop their physical, mental, and social skills, and to win games (although winning is by no means the most important thing).

A—AFFECTION: An effective lacrosse coach has genuine care and concern for the health and welfare of the players and does not push them beyond their limits.

C—CHARACTER: An effective lacrosse coach knows the importance of being a good role model for players and strives always to treat everyone with respect and value.

H—HUMOR: An effective lacrosse coach always maintains a sense of humor, striving to make practices fun and enjoyable, and keeping players' mistakes in perspective.

Glossary

Anatomy: The study of the structures of organisms.

Centrifugal: Describing the force that tends to impel a thing outward from a center of rotation.

Check (v.): To block the progress of.

Cleats: Wedges projecting from the bottom of a shoe to provide grip.

Compression bandage: A bandage that holds a swollen joint or muscle tightly to reduce the swelling.

Concussion: A jarring injury of the brain.

Contusion: Severe bruising, accompanied by internal bleeding.

Crosier: Staff resembling a shepherd's crook, carried by bishops and abbots as a symbol of office.

Debilitating: Weakening.

Dislocation: An injury in which a joint in the body is wrenched or knocked out of its normal position.

Etiquette: Correct behavior, as prescribed by rule or custom.

Fracture: A break or split in a bone.

Hamstrings: The group of three large muscles set at the back of the thigh, which are used to flex the leg.

Ligament: A short band of tough body tissue, which connects bones or holds together joints.

Overuse injury: An injury caused by repeating the same action many times.

Physiology: A branch of biology, dealing with the processes of living organisms.

Posthumously: Following or occurring after death.

Quadriceps: A large, four-part muscle on the front of the thigh, which is used to extend the leg.

Rotator cuff: The group of muscles holding the shoulder joint in place, enabling the rotational movement of the arm.

Spasm: An involuntary and abnormal muscular contraction.

Splint: Material or device used to protect and immobilize a body part.

Spotter: The person who assists a gymnast in making a technique during training.

Stamina: Staying power, endurance.

Further Information

USEFUL WEB SITES

For a comprehensive site on lacrosse history, tips, drills, equipment, and jobs in the sport, try: www.laxlinks.com

Major League Lacrosse: www.majorleaguelacrosse.com

National Lacrosse League organization: www.nll.com

For younger players, this site contains lacrosse news, team rankings, and articles: www.youthlacrosseusa.com

The Web sites listed on this page were active at the time of publication. The publisher is not responsible for Web sites that have changed their address or discontinued operation since the date of publication. The publisher will review and update the Web sites upon each reprint.

FURTHER READING

American Sport Education Program. *Coaching Youth Lacrosse.* Champaign, Illinois: Human Kinetics, 2002.

Crossingham, John. *Lacrosse in Action.* New York: Crabtree Publishing, 2003.

Hinkson, Jim and Ben Hinkson. *Lacrosse Fundamentals.* Woodside, California: Warwick Publishing, 1993.

Micheli, Lyle J. *The Sports Medicine Bible.* New York: HarperPerennial, 1995.

Tucker, Janine and Maryalice Yakutchik. *The Baffled Parent's Guide to Coaching Girls' Lacrosse.* Camden, Maine: Ragged Mountain Press/McGraw-Hill, 2003.

Vennum, Thomas Jr. *American Indian Lacrosse: Little Brother of War.* Washington, D.C.: Smithsonian Institution Press, 1994.

THE AUTHOR

Lisa McCoy, a former cheerleader, is a freelance writer and editor living in Washington State. Her work covers a wide range of industries, and she has published more than a dozen titles. For a recent short story, she garnered an Honorable Mention in the L. Ron Hubbard's Writers of the Future contest, and she is now at work on a fantasy novel.

THE CONSULTANTS

Susan Saliba, Ph.D., is a senior associate athletic trainer and a clinical instructor at the University of Virginia in Charlottesville, Virginia. A certified athletic trainer and licensed physical therapist, Dr. Saliba provides sports medicine care, including prevention, treatment, and rehabilitation for the varsity athletes at the University. Dr. Saliba holds dual appointments as an Assistant Professor in the Curry School of Education and the Department of Orthopaedic Surgery. She is a member of the National Athletic Trainers' Association's Educational Executive Committee and its Clinical Education Committee.

Eric Small, M.D., a Harvard-trained sports medicine physician, is a nationally recognized expert in the field of sports injuries, nutritional supplements, and weight management programs. He is author of *Kids & Sports* (2002) and is Assistant Clinical Professor of Pediatrics, Orthopedics, and Rehabilitation Medicine at Mount Sinai School of Medicine in New York. He is also Director of the Sports Medicine Center for Young Athletes at Blythedale Children's Hospital in Valhalla, New York. Dr. Small has served on the American Academy of Pediatrics Committee on Sports Medicine for the past six years, where he develops national policy regarding children's medical issues and sports.

Index

DATE DUE